World of Wonder

EARTH and the UNIVERSE

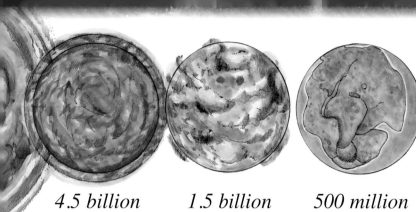

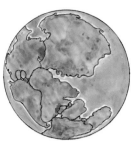

4.5 billion years ago

1.5 billion years ago

500 million years ago

200 million years ago

135 million years ago

Our home planet, Earth, formed 4.5 billion years ago. Millions of years ago, there was one giant continent surrounded by ocean. Then the land split up and very slowly moved to where it is now.

The Earth today

© The Salariya Book Company Ltd MMVIII
No part of this publication may be reproduced in whole or in part, or stored in a retrieval system, or transmitted in any form or by any means, electronic, mechanical, photocopying, recording, or otherwise, without written permission of the publisher. For information regarding permission, write to: salariya@salariya.com

Published in Great Britain in 2008 by
The Salariya Book Company Ltd
25 Marlborough Place, Brighton BN1 1UB

ISBN-13: 978-0-531-24025-0 (lib. bdg.)   978-0-531-23821-9 (pbk.)
ISBN-10: 0-531-24025-8 (lib. bdg.)   0-531-23821-0 (pbk.)

All rights reserved.
Published in 2009 in the United States by Children's Press
An imprint of Scholastic Inc.

A CIP catalog record for this book is available from the Library of Congress.

Printed and bound in China.
Printed on paper from sustainable sources.

Author: Ian Graham studied applied physics at the City University, London. He then obtained a postgraduate degree in journalism, specializing in science and technology. Since becoming a freelance author and journalist, he has written more than one hundred children's nonfiction books.

Artists: Julian Baker, Mark Bergin, Bill Donohoe, Nick Hewetson, Carolyn Scrace, Tony Townsend, Rob Walker

Editor: Stephen Haynes

Editorial assistants: Rob Walker, Tanya Kant

PAPER FROM
SUSTAINABLE
FORESTS

World of Wonder

Earth and the Universe

by Ian Graham

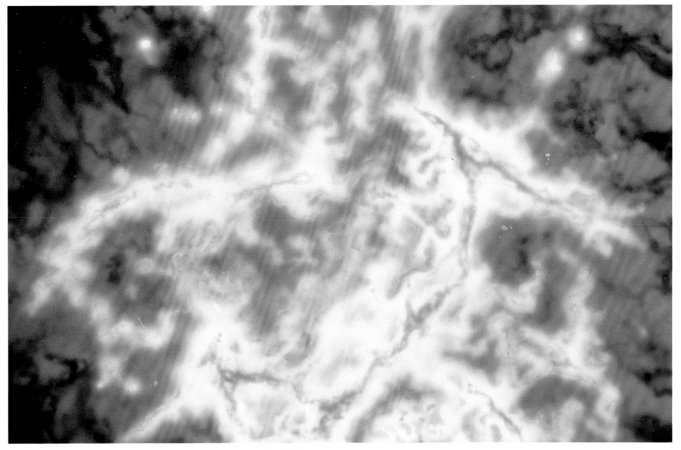

children's press®

An Imprint of Scholastic Inc.

NEW YORK • TORONTO • LONDON • AUCKLAND • SYDNEY

MEXICO CITY • NEW DELHI • HONG KONG

DANBURY, CONNECTICUT

Contents

Where Are We in the Universe?

We live on a small planet called Earth. It travels around an ordinary star, the sun. The sun is just one of hundreds of billions of stars in our part of the **universe**. This book is about our home planet and its place in the universe.

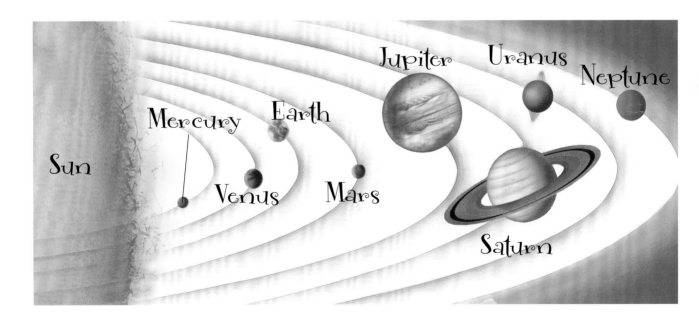

Sun

Mercury

Venus

Earth

Mars

Jupiter

Saturn

Uranus

Neptune

Our solar system

Earth is the third of eight planets that **orbit** (travel around) the sun.

What Causes Earthquakes?

The Earth is made up of layers. The main layers are the crust on the outside, the mantle underneath it, and the core in the center.

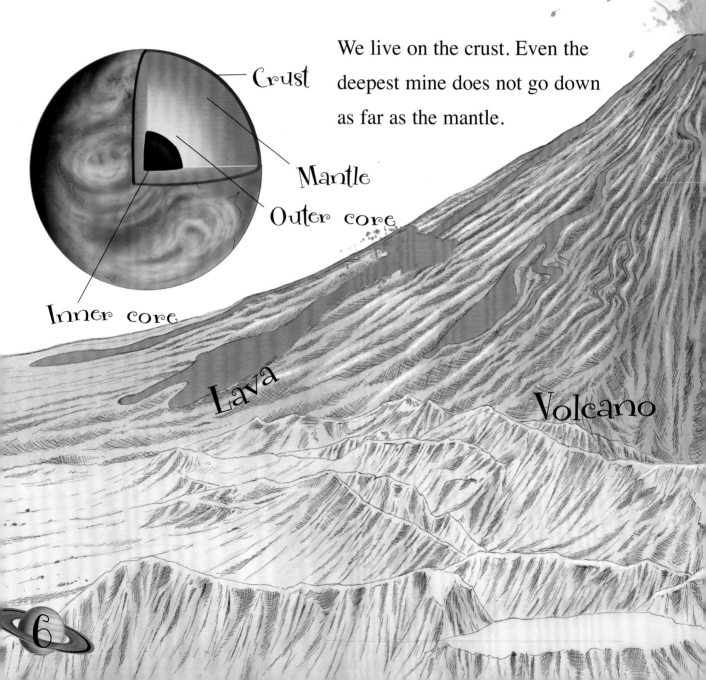

We live on the crust. Even the deepest mine does not go down as far as the mantle.

Crust

Mantle

Outer core

Inner core

Lava

Volcano

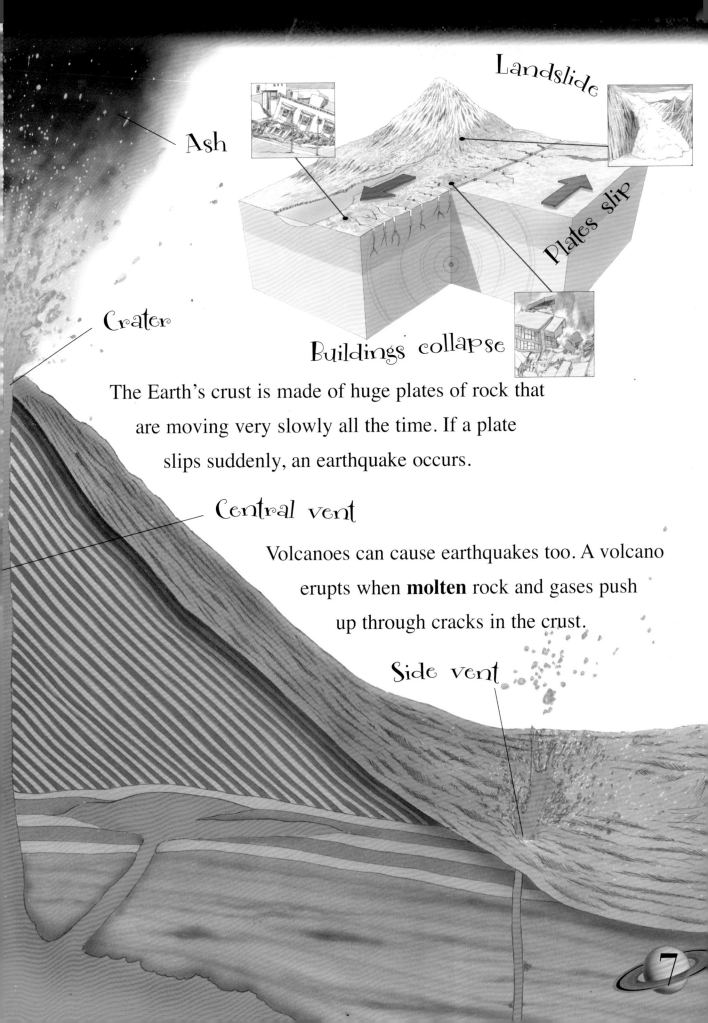

Ash

Landslide

Crater

Plates slip

Buildings collapse

The Earth's crust is made of huge plates of rock that are moving very slowly all the time. If a plate slips suddenly, an earthquake occurs.

Central vent

Volcanoes can cause earthquakes too. A volcano erupts when **molten** rock and gases push up through cracks in the crust.

Side vent

What's the Highest Point on Earth?

The highest point on Earth is the top of Mount Everest. It stands 29,035 feet high on the border of Nepal and Tibet. Mount Everest is part of a huge mountain range called the Himalayas.

Mount Everest

29,035 feet

Sea level

Mauna Kea

33,000 feet

Mount Everest

The **summit** of Mount Everest is the highest place above sea level. But a mountain in Hawaii called Mauna Kea is even taller than Everest. Measured from sea level, Mauna Kea is only 13,796 feet high. But more than half of Mauna Kea lies under the sea. From the ocean floor, Mauna Kea rises almost 33,000 feet.

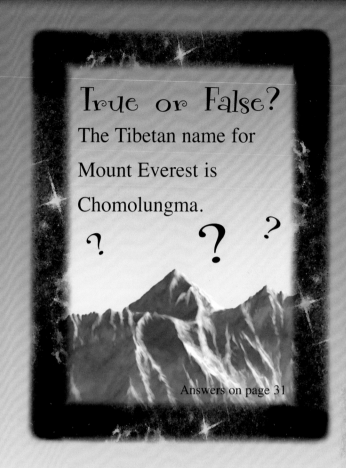

True or False?
The Tibetan name for Mount Everest is Chomolungma.
? ? ?

Answers on page 31

Himalayas

What's the Deepest Place on Earth?

The deepest place on the Earth's surface is at the bottom of a valley under the Pacific Ocean. It is called the Mariana Trench because it lies near the Mariana Islands. The trench is 1,585 miles long. The deepest part of it is called Challenger Deep. It's about 6.8 miles below sea level.

How deep have humans gone?

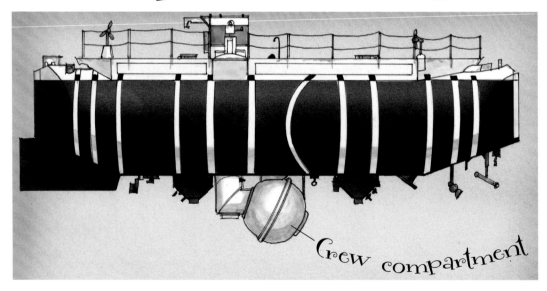

Crew compartment

In 1960, the American vessel *Trieste* dived to the bottom of the Mariana Trench. It had two people on board. So far, this is still the deepest ever manned dive.

10

1 mile

Grand Canyon

10 miles

1.9 miles

Olympus Mons

True or False?
70% of the world is covered by water.

? ? ?

Answers on page 31

The Grand Canyon is the largest canyon in the USA, though it is not the deepest. It is 1 mile deep and 10 miles wide on average. The crater at the top of Olympus Mons on the planet Mars (see pages 22–23) is nearly twice as deep and nearly five times as wide.

What's the Longest River?

The longest river in the world is probably the Nile in Africa. It is 4,160 miles long. But the Amazon River in South America is wider than the Nile and carries more water. Some scientists think it might even be longer than the Nile— it is very difficult to measure rivers exactly.

People have depended on the Nile for water since the time of the pharaohs, thousands of years ago.

Pyramids along the Nile

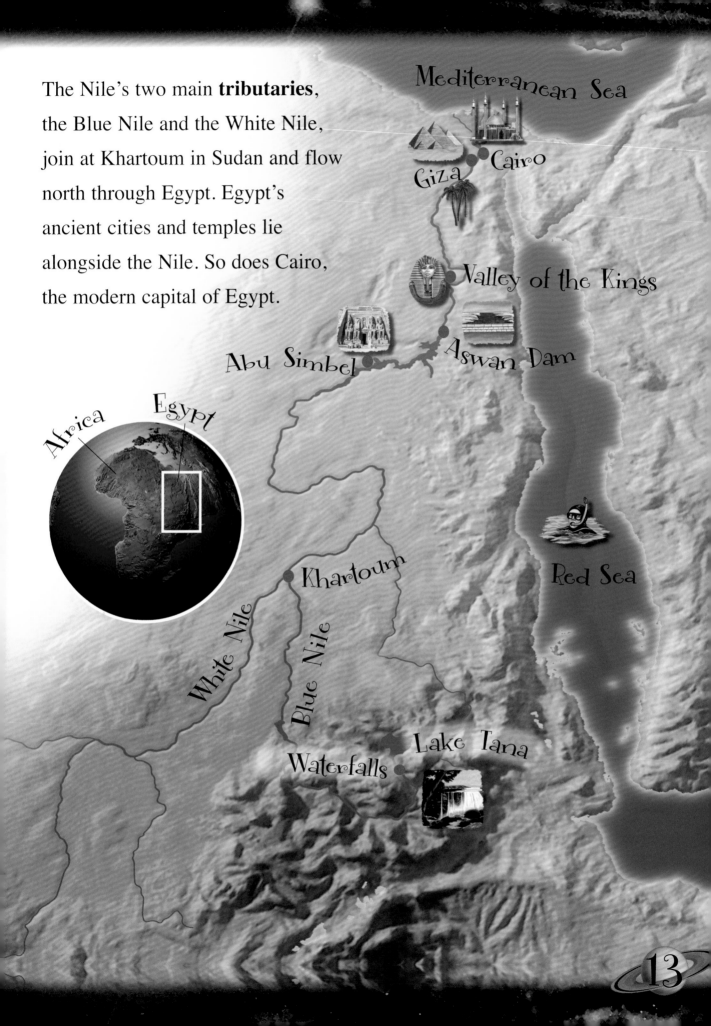

The Nile's two main **tributaries**, the Blue Nile and the White Nile, join at Khartoum in Sudan and flow north through Egypt. Egypt's ancient cities and temples lie alongside the Nile. So does Cairo, the modern capital of Egypt.

Mediterranean Sea

Giza
Cairo

Valley of the Kings

Abu Simbel

Aswan Dam

Africa

Egypt

Red Sea

Khartoum

White Nile

Blue Nile

Lake Tana

Waterfalls

13

Thermosphere

Satellites

Space Shuttle

Mesosphere

Meteors (shooting stars)

Stratosphere

High-altitude balloons

Ozone layer

In orbit

The Space Shuttle orbits the Earth usually at about 180 to 250 miles above the ground. Even at this great height, there is just enough air to slow the spacecraft down a little.

Troposphere

Clouds

14

What Is the Atmosphere?

The atmosphere is the blanket of air that surrounds the Earth. Most of the air is in the lower part of the atmosphere. Higher up, the atmosphere gets thinner and thinner until there is none at all. At 60 miles above the ground the atmosphere is very thin, but there is still some air. You'd have to use a spacecraft to go higher than 50 miles.

No other planet in the solar system has an atmosphere like ours. Earth's atmosphere has five main layers. From the ground up, they are the troposphere, stratosphere, mesosphere, thermosphere, and exosphere. Most of the clouds and weather are in the lowest layer, the troposphere.

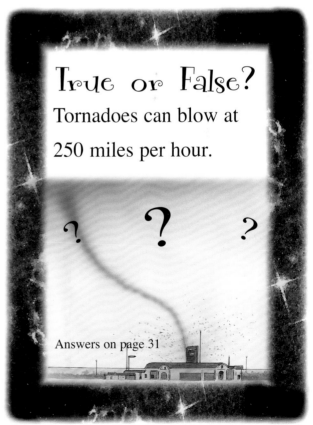

True or False?

Tornadoes can blow at 250 miles per hour.

? ? ?

Answers on page 31

15

Is Earth a Large Planet or a Small Planet?

Earth is part of the **solar system**. The solar system is the sun and everything that goes around it. The largest **planet** in our solar system is Jupiter; 1,321 Earths would fit inside it. Jupiter is a type of planet called a "gas giant." It is mainly gas and liquid. Nearly all of it is hydrogen and helium—the same stuff that makes up the sun.

True or False?

Pluto is a planet.

? ? ? ?

Pluto

Answers on page 31

The four planets closest to the sun are all small and solid.

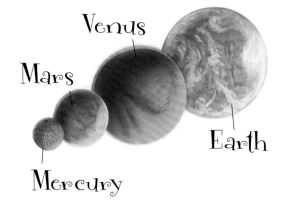

Venus

Mars

Mercury

Earth

Mercury was the smallest planet until faraway Pluto was discovered in 1930. Pluto is even smaller—but is it a planet?

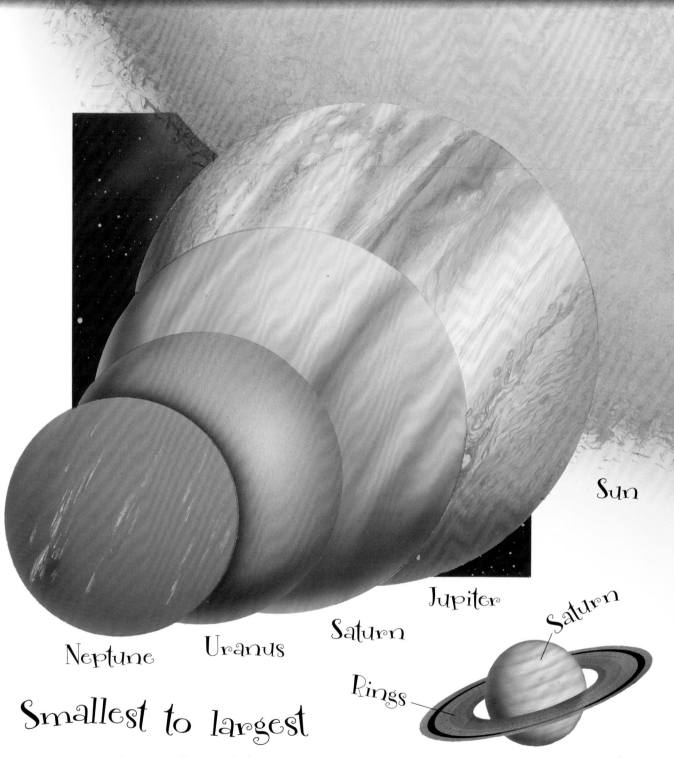

Sun

Jupiter

Saturn

Neptune

Uranus

Saturn

Rings

Smallest to largest

Neptune is the smallest of the gas giants, followed by Uranus, Saturn, and Jupiter. Saturn has rings made from tiny pieces of ice and dust.

The pictures on these two pages show the planets of our solar system in order of size. The order in which they orbit the sun is shown on page 5.

What's the Hottest Planet?

Mercury is the closest planet to the Sun. Does that make it the hottest? No! The next planet, Venus, is the hottest. Unlike Mercury, Venus has a thick atmosphere that traps heat from the sun. Its surface sizzles at about 896°F—that's hot enough to melt lead.

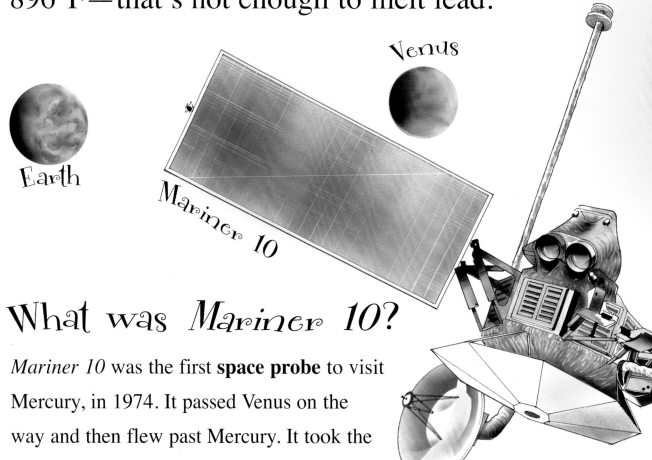

Venus

Earth

Mariner 10

What was Mariner 10?

Mariner 10 was the first **space probe** to visit Mercury, in 1974. It passed Venus on the way and then flew past Mercury. It took the first close-up photographs of both planets.

Venus

Venus is nearly as big as Earth. It is
the brightest planet in the night sky,
even brighter than any star. It is
easiest to see just before sunrise and
just after sunset, so it has been
called both the Morning Star and
the Evening Star.

Sun

Mercury

Mercury

Mercury is not much bigger than the
Moon. It even looks like the Moon.

Which Planet Has the Longest Day?

A day is the length of time from one sunrise to the next sunrise. Because a planet spins, the sun seems to rise and cross the sky each day. A day on Earth is 24 hours long. The planet with the longest day of all is tiny Mercury. A day on Mercury is 176 Earth days long. Venus has the second-longest day, lasting almost 117 Earth days.

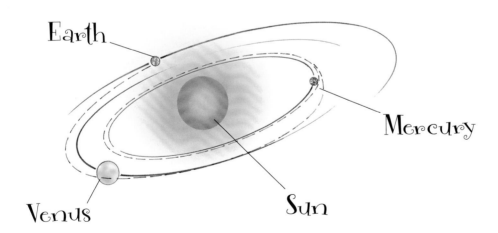

Earth

Mercury

Venus

Sun

Average distances from the sun:

Earth: 93 million miles

Venus: 67 million miles

Mercury: 36 million miles

Which planet has the shortest day?

Jupiter, the biggest planet, spins so fast that it has the shortest day in the solar system – only 9 hours, 55 minutes. Its fast spin and heat from its interior whip up powerful storms. Jupiter's Great Red Spot is a storm more than twice the size of the Earth!

True or False?

Mercury, like Earth, has one **moon**.

Answers on page 31

Jupiter

—— Great Red Spot

What's the Highest Volcano in the Solar System?

The highest volcano in the solar system is on the planet Mars. It's a mountain called Olympus Mons. It's 17 miles high and 375 miles across.

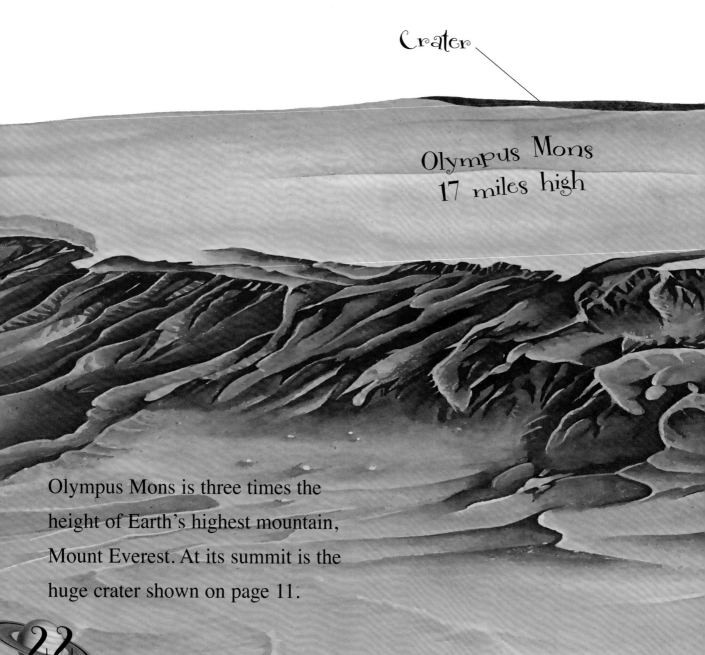

Crater

Olympus Mons
17 miles high

Olympus Mons is three times the height of Earth's highest mountain, Mount Everest. At its summit is the huge crater shown on page 11.

Mount Everest
5.5 miles high

Mariner 9

How was Olympus Mons discovered?

The *Mariner 9* space probe discovered Olympus Mons in 1971. Its cameras saw the volcano looming up through the dust thrown up by a huge storm.

Only part of Olympus Mons is shown here. To show all of it at this scale, the book would have to be about 11 feet wide.

How Far Away Is Our Nearest Star?

Our nearest star is the sun, about 93 million miles away. The next nearest is called Proxima Centauri. It's about 4.2 **light years** away from our sun. A light year is the distance light travels in one year—nearly 25 trillion miles.

Our sun   Alpha Centauri A   Proxima Centauri

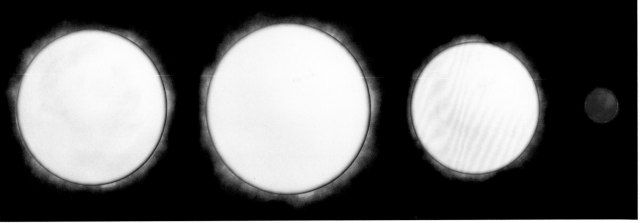

Alpha Centauri B

Our sun is a lone star. It travels through space on its own. Some stars travel in pairs or groups. Proxima Centauri is one of three stars that travel together.

The other two stars are called Alpha Centauri A and Alpha Centauri B. These two are roughly the same size as the sun. Proxima Centauri is much smaller.

Why are there telescopes in space?

Hubble Space Telescope

The haze and clouds of the Earth's atmosphere make it difficult to see clearly into space. **Telescopes** in space can make sharper pictures. The Hubble Space Telescope was launched in 1990. It orbits the Earth 380 miles above the ground.

Powerful telescopes on Earth use curved mirrors inside a heavy frame to collect light from space.

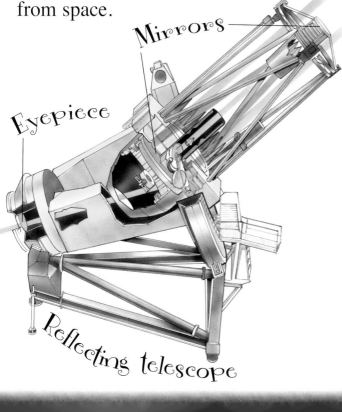

Mirrors

Eyepiece

Reflecting telescope

True or False?

The nearest planet outside our solar system is 10.5 light years away.

?

?

?

Answers on page 31

Energy pouring from the core

Core

Photosphere

Prominences

How Hot Is the Sun?

The center of the sun is amazingly hot—about 27,000,000°F. Energy pours out of the sun's core into the outer layers of the sun. These layers are cooler, but still very hot. The part of the sun that we can see is called the photosphere. Its temperature is about 10,000°F.

What is solar wind?

Solar wind is a stream of particles pouring out from the sun. The sun boils with huge explosions called "flares" and tongues of gas called "prominences." Some particles fly out so fast that they escape into space. The solar wind streams out in all directions at up to 560 miles every second.

True or False?

A solar flare can affect radio waves on Earth.

Answers on page 31

How Big Is Our Galaxy?

Stars are not spread out evenly throughout the Universe. They clump together in vast collections of stars called **galaxies**. The sun is one of about 200 billion stars that form a galaxy called the Milky Way. The Milky Way is about 100,000 light years wide.

There are three main types or shapes of galaxies: spiral, elliptical, and irregular. Our galaxy, the Milky Way, is a spiral galaxy.

The Milky Way
A spiral galaxy

We live about 26,000 light years from the center of the Milky Way.

True or False?

Light cannot escape from a **black hole**.

? ? ?

Answers on page 31

Spiral galaxy

Irregular galaxy

Useful Words

Atmosphere The gas that surrounds a planet, moon, or star. Earth's atmosphere is made from a mixture of gases called air.

Black hole An object formed when a giant star collapses. The gravity in a black hole is so strong that nothing can escape—not even light.

Galaxy A collection of millions or billions of stars traveling through space together.

Light year The distance light travels in one year—almost 25 trillion miles.

Molten Melted by heat. The molten rock that comes out of a volcano is called lava.

Moon A smaller object that orbits a planet. Earth has only one moon.

Orbit To go around and around a planet, star, or other object in space.

Planet A large ball of rock or gas that orbits a star.

Solar system The sun and everything that orbits the sun.

Space probe An unmanned spacecraft sent to study planets, moons, or other objects in space.

Summit The top of a mountain.

Telescope An instrument for making faraway things look nearer.

Tributary A stream or river that flows into a larger river and becomes part of it.

Universe Everything there is, everywhere.

Answers

Page 9 TRUE! The Tibetan name for Mount Everest is Chomolungma, which means "Goddess Mother of the World" or "Goddess Mother of the Valley."

Page 11 TRUE! The oceans and seas cover 70% of the Earth's surface with salty water.

Page 15 TRUE! A tornado is a column of air spinning very fast. The wind in the most powerful tornadoes can blow at 250 mph or more. The whole tornado can move across the ground at more than 60 mph.

Page 16 FALSE! When Pluto was first discovered, it was called a planet. But when more objects like Pluto were found, astronomers decided to call them "dwarf planets." In 2006 it was officially decided that Pluto was not a proper planet. Mercury is once again the smallest planet in the solar system.

Page 21 FALSE! Mercury and Venus have no moons, Earth has one, and Mars has two. The four outer planets, the gas giants, have more than 150 moons.

Page 25 TRUE! More than 200 planets have been discovered orbiting other stars. The nearest is called Epsilon Eridani B, because it orbits a star called Epsilon Eridani. It's about 10.5 light years away.

Page 27 TRUE! A solar flare sends out a burst of energy and particles that causes radio interference on Earth. The strongest flares can cause power outages.

Page 29 TRUE! The biggest stars end their days by collapsing and forming a strange object called a black hole. Its gravity is so strong that nothing, not even light, can escape. There may be a black hole at the center of some galaxies, including ours.

In the 1890s, U.S. astronomer Percival Lowell thought he saw canals built by Martians on Mars. When space probes visited Mars, they found no canals or Martians!

Index

(Illustrations are shown in **bold type**.)